The

ABC's

Of Texas
Wildflowers

The

ABC's

Of Texas
Wildflowers

Text by Glenna Gardiner Grimmer
Illustrations by Mary Jo Laughlin

TABLE OF
CONTENTS

With special thanks to ...

My mother whose enthusiasm for life and love of nature have been guiding influences in my life.

Harold Laughlin, Administrative Director of Heard Natural Science Museum of McKinney, for his patient reading and re-reading of my manuscript.

Joan Shelley, Coordinator of Talented and Gifted Children's Program of the Carrollton-Farmers Branch Independent School District, for her whole-hearted support.

Montrue Doty, fourth grade teacher in the C-FB ISD, for her generous help.

Mary Jo Laughlin, wildflower artist, who added her extensive knowledge as well as her artistic talents to the illustrations.

— *Glenna Gardiner Grimmer*

FOREWORD

THE ABC'S OF TEXAS WILDFLOWERS is an introduction to the wonderful world of wildflowers. Even the smallest blossoms are worth examining. Wildflowers grow everywhere — in fields, vacant lots and alleyways — wherever there is a patch of ground. Hopefully this book will begin a lifelong study of one of Texas' most beautiful natural resources — *wildflowers.*

The twenty-six *flowers* in the book were chosen because they are common to many areas of the state and can be easily identified. They are in alphabetical order to assist you in remembering names. A wildflower, once identified, becomes a "friend" for life. When familiar with this limited number, I hope you will want to explore the many other wildflowers *native* to the State of Texas.

Plant families are like families of people — members have *characteristics* in common yet may be surprisingly different in appearance. Common individual and family names have been used for easier reading. More detailed texts can supply *scientific names* and technical information.

Blooming times for each flower may vary from area to area depending on climate and soil conditions, and this should always be considered when looking for wildflowers.

Words in italic type are in the glossary at the back of the book. Only names of specific flowers have been capitalized. For instance, "aster" is not capitalized, whereas, "Smooth Aster" is.

Hopefully THE ABC'S OF TEXAS WILDFLOWERS will begin a lifelong adventure.

— *Glenna Gardiner Grimmer*

mclaughlin © 1982

ASTER

Family: Composite
Blooms: Summer - Fall

Asters are common roadside flowers and are somewhat like their daisy cousins in appearance. The blossoms are usually smaller with many petals around a yellow center. As with most members of the Composite Family, the center of the aster is made up of small *disk flowers* and the petals are called *ray flowers.* Asters often close at night waiting for the sun to open them each day. Leaves of the aster grow *alternately* on the *stem,* and there are fewer leaves on the plant when the flowers are in bloom. Asters make up a very large group within the Composite Family. One group of asters is called "golden asters," because their ray flowers as well as the disk flowers are yellow. Some golden asters have small flowerheads common to asters — others have wider, more daisy-like blooms. The other group of asters may have white, pink or purple flowers — the most common being the purple-flowered aster. Aster names include Smooth Aster, Narrow-leaved Aster, Small-leaved Aster and Broad-leaved Aster. Such common names are helpful in identifying the flowers. This is important because there are so many kinds of asters and it is sometimes difficult to tell them apart.

mclaughlin
© 1982

BLUEBONNET

Family: Legume
Blooms: March - May

Lovely bluebonnets brighten the Central Texas landscape each spring creating a carpet of blue. The blossom is made up of small flowers growing on a single *stalk*. The stalk with *flowerets* is called a *raceme*. The flowerets look like little faces under bonnets. The faces are white near the top of the flower; a few wine-colored faces may be found near the bottom of the bloom.

Some texts refer to this family as the "Pea Family." "Lupine," which also means "pea," is from the Latin word *"lupus,"* which means "wolf." Many years ago it was believed that lupines, such as the bluebonnet, *devoured nutrients* in the soil. As a matter of fact, bluebonnets improve the soil by supplying nitrogen through *nodules* on the plant's root system.

Oblong leaflets grow in *clusters* of five with either rounded or slightly pointed tips. This kind of leaf arrangement is called a *compound leaf.*

Bluebonnet seeds have a hard shell that must be cracked in order for the seeds to *sprout.* Sometimes the seeds will stay in the ground for years before the shells are cracked and the plants begin to grow.

There are five kinds of bluebonnets in Texas and all are considered the state flower.

mclaughlin © 1982

CONE-FLOWER

Family: Composite
Blooms: Spring - Summer

Cone-flowers are easily recognized because their centers stand up like cones above the petals which often droop downward toward the center. The center *disk flowers* are usually brown and are covered with a red-brown *chaff* or *scale.*

The blossoms grow on the ends of the *stems* giving the flower an erect, upright appearance. Leaves grow *alternately* on the stem; some are shiny, some are hairy. Most are *oblong* in shape.

Cone-flowers are among our most beautiful wildflowers and are easily *cultivated* in the garden. They may be pink, purple, white, red, yellow or combinations of red and yellow.

Pictured is a Purple Cone-flower. The blossom is two to three and one-half inches across and the plant grows to a height of one to three feet. There are usually ten to twelve petals or *ray flowers* around the center.

Indians often used roots of the Purple Cone-flower to heal burns and other injuries. They are still used today in making certain types of medicine.

DOGWOOD

Family: Dogwood
Blooms: March - April

The woods of East Texas and the southern states are brightened by lovely dogwood trees in early spring. Four wide, white *floral* leaves, called *bracts,* surround small green flowers. The white bracts of the dogwood are often called petals, but they are not. The petal-like bracts have *notched* tips usually *tinged* with brown — sometimes shaded with pink.

Clusters of small greenish-white flowers appear on the bare tree in early spring, then the floral bracts and leaves add their springtime beauty. The tree may grow to a height of thirty-eight feet.

Because the floral bracts of the dogwood are so beautiful, they are often broken off the tree for indoor arrangements. This is not a good thing to do because the beauty is short lived and such action damages the tree. A much better way to enjoy the beautiful, simple design of the dogwood is to draw or paint a picture of the white bracts surrounding the green center flowers. This is an easy project for a beginning artist.

Dye, *quinine* and tools are some of the products made from the bark and wood of the dogwood tree.

mclaughlin
© 1982

ERYNGO

Family: Carrot
Blooms: August - September

Eryngo is so often misnamed as "purple thistle," that it is frequently listed in wildflower books as "false purple thistle," but it is a member of the Carrot Family. The gray-green *foliage* turns bright purple in September dotting fields and roadsides with beauty.

The flowers can be dried for wintertime decorations by hanging them upside down in a dark room or closet for several weeks. Although still beautiful, some of the purple color will fade. Care must be taken in handling, however, because of the many sharp-pointed leaves and *bracts* on the plant. Of course, no wildflower should be cut from public property or from private property without permission.

Leaves grow in *clusters* on sturdy *stalks*. As the plant grows, other *stems fork* from these clusters with short-stemmed flowers growing in the forks. Floral leaves (bracts) cluster on top of the *oblong*, barrel-shaped flowers. Eryngos grow to a height of one to three feet.

mclaughlin
© 1982

FLEABANE

Family: Composite
Blooms: February - May

The little fleabane is common along roadsides of Texas and the southern states waving *fragile* blossoms in spring breezes. One must stop and examine the fleabane to know it from other white flowers especially the white-flowered aster. The fleabane may be recognized by the many, many fine petals (sometimes as many as 150) around a yellow center. And fleabanes usually bloom earlier in the spring than do asters. The small *flowerheads* of the fleabanes are somewhat flat, and each plant has numerous branches with many flowers on each *stem.*

Remember that the center is made up of small *"disk flowers"* and the thread-like petals are *"ray flowers."* A magnifying glass will help one see the tiny disk flowers in fleabanes and other members of the Composite Family.

The leaves of the fleabane grow *opposite* each other and are *lance* shaped. slightly pointed, sometimes with *saw-tooth* edges. The flowerheads of most fleabanes are about three-fourths of an inch across and the plant grows to a height of one and one-half to three feet.

Names of fleabanes include Philadelphia Fleabane and Daisy Fleabane.

mcloughlin © 1982

GOLDENROD

Family: Composite
Blooms: Late summer

Goldenrods grow best in damp places and there are many kinds *native* to Texas. Small yellow flowers bloom along a slender *stem* that looks like a wand or rod that has been dipped in gold. There are only a few yellow *ray flowers* on each *floweret* surrounding the yellow *disk flowers.*

Leaves of the goldenrod may be smooth or rough — often hairy and they grow *alternately* on the stem.

Many people think the goldenrod causes hay fever, but it does not. The *pollen* is too moist and sticky to float freely through the air and cause problems.

Goldenrod plants make good *forage* food for cattle and the leaves can be used to make a tea. However, you should never taste any leaf or plant that is unknown to you. Oil from goldenrod leaves is sometimes used in medicine as a tonic. Many plants were used by our forefathers in this way, and some, like the goldenrod, are still considered beneficial.

Although goldenrods may be easily recognized as a group, it is often hard to tell one kind of goldenrod from another. Some goldenrod names are Tall Goldenrod, Dwarf Goldenrod and Stiff Goldenrod.

mclaughlin
© 1982

HORSEMINT

Family: Mint
Blooms: May - August

When in bloom, a horsemint sometimes looks like a small tower of flowers. *Clusters* of small flowers grow around a sturdy *stem*. Each pretty cluster is surrounded by colorful *floral bracts*. As the plant grows, another *whorled* cluster of flowers is added to the end of the stem. Some blossoms have as many as ten clusters on one stalk.

A crushed leaf quickly tells that this plant, which may grow to a height of one to three freet, is a member of the Mint Family. It has a *pungent,* not unpleasant, odor although it is not as sweet as peppermint. Oil from horsemint is sometimes used in making perfume.

Horsemint blossoms are very attractive to bees, although the plant does not add to the flavor of honey made by bees that gather its nectar. Butterflies also like horsemint blossoms.

There are Purple, Green and Lemon Horsemint, and each kind has varying shades of these colors in its flowers.

INDIAN BLANKET

Family: Composite
Blooms: April - June

Indian Blankets are among our most beautiful and widespread wildflowers. The bright red and yellow of the blossom are colors that might be woven into an Indian blanket. Another name for this flower is firewheel—also a good name because the rusty-red petals are often tipped with flame yellow.

Indian Blankets grow in many places — roadsides, fields, vacant lots and prairies. They are easily *cultivated* for garden blooming. The *solitary* blooms grow on stiff, upright *stems*. This beautiful flower makes an excellent flower for indoor arrangements, but like all wildflowers should not be cut from public places but left for everyone to enjoy. It is this long-lasting quality, as well as the colorful beauty of the bloom, that makes it such a good flower for home gardens.

The plant grows to a height of one to one and one-half feet and each blossom is two to three inches across with ten to twenty broad, three *lobed* petals. Leaves grow *alternately* on the stem; the upper ones are *lance* shaped; the lower ones are *oblong* with lobed or *saw-toothed* edges.

mclaughlin
© 1982

JASMINE, CAROLINA

Family: Logania
Blooms: January - April

One of the loveliest wildflowers of the woods of East Texas is Carolina Jasmine. Many books refer to it as "jessamine." The jasmine vine, with thin, lance-like leaves, grows on fences and even into the tops of tall trees. When there has been enough rain, this woodland beauty seems to grow everywhere with trailing vines and bright yellow flowers. Sometimes the vines are so high that only a fallen blossom and lovely fragrance tell that a jasmine is blooming nearby.

The yellow flowers are shaped like small bells with five deep *lobes*. They truly ring in the growing season because the jasmine is among the earliest of spring bloomers. The flower is one to one and one-half inches long and one inch across.

An easy-to-grow garden variety of Carolina Jasmine is available, and this lovely flower can be enjoyed by everyone. The wildflower blooms only once in early spring — the *domestic* jasmine blooms several times during the year. Also, the wild variety may lose all or most of its leaves in winter while the cultivated jasmine is *evergreen.*

mclaughlin
© 1982

KISSES

Family: Evening Primrose
Blooms: March - May

This flower is also called "wild-honeysuckle" although it is not a honeysuckle at all but a member of the Evening Primrose Family. The sweet fragrance of kisses is reason enough to call it a honeysuckle.

The flowers grow on slender, erect stems or *spikes* rising above the *foliage*. Each small flower has four petals which grow on the upper side of the blossom giving it a lopsided appearance. Eight *stamens* and a long *style* droop below the petals like whiskers.

Usually only two or three *flowerets* are open at one time. Opening in the late afternoon or evening, the white flowers turn to shades of pink as they are warmed by the morning sun.

The plant usually grows to a height of one to three feet; leaves grow *alternately* on the stem and sometimes have *saw-toothed* edges.

There are several kinds of kisses, also called gaura, and it is difficult to tell them apart. Two common ones are Prairie Gaura and Large-flowered Gaura.

mclaughlin
© 1982

LANTANA

Family: Vervain
Blooms: May - December

The small flowers of the lantana grow in flat *clusters* at the ends of stiff *stems*. The entire flower is usually one and one-half inches across; each *floweret* in the cluster is only about one-fourth inch across — a perfect little flower.

The plant is a small *shrub* usually growing to a height of about three feet but it can grow as tall as seven feet. Lantanas are often planted for garden blooming. Years ago authorities did not consider lantana a true wildflower, but the plant has become so common without being planted that in certain areas of Texas some kinds are considered *naturalized* plants.

Flowerets in the clusters are orange, red, yellow, pink or vivid combinations of these colors. The bright green leaves are lance-shaped with saw-toothed edges. They are rough textured and grow opposite each other on the stem. The full name of this flower is West Indian Lantana.

molaughlin
© 1982

MEXICAN HAT

Family: Composite
Blooms: May - November

This beautiful wildflower looks like its name. Brownish-red, velvety-*textured* petals, often yellow tipped, turn downward from a cone-shaped center. In some flowers the ray petals may be entirely yellow. The center *"disk"* resembles the tall crown of a hat (it may be two inches high), the petals are the floppy brim.

Solitary flowers grow on the ends of upright *stems* rising above the *foliage* as though to tip their hats to passersby. The center is grayish-green before the small brown *disk flowers* appear. The stem of the plant, which grows to a height of about two and one-half feet, is slender, branching from the base. Each flower has four to ten *ray flowers* around the center.

Mexican Hats have long-lasting qualities as cut flowers. It is therefore fortunate that they are easily grown for home gardens since wildflowers are for everyone to enjoy and should not be taken from fields where they grow. The plant grows in *abundance* over much of Texas.

Mexican Hats are related to cone flowers and Blackeyed Susans.

mclaughlin © 1982

NIGHTSHADE

Family: Potato
Blooms: May - October

There are several kinds of nightshades including White Nightshade, Buffalo-bur and Purple Nightshade. Another common one is called Silver-leafed Nightshade because the leaves have a silvery *hue* to their rather pale green color. Most nightshades have *spiny stems*. These plants grow to heights of about two feet.

Although a member of the Potato Family, there is nothing good to eat about the nightshade — not even the yellowish fruit called "tomatillo" or "little tomato" that appears after the flowers are gone. Some authorities say the plant is *poisonous*.

The star-shaped flowers have five petals and bloom on short stems. The Purple Nightshade is a bluish purple color and the yellow center is made up of five *stamen* and one *pistil* which stand above the petals. The stamens of a flower bears the *pollen* which unites with an *ovule* in the pistil, making it possible for the flower to reproduce. Stamens and pistils are present in most flowers, but they are not always as easily seen as in the nightshade. Another name for Purple Nightshade is "Trompillo."

molaughlin
©
1982

ONION, WILD

Family: Lily
Blooms: April - May

Lawns and open spaces are often dotted with the pinkish-white flowers of Wild Onion. The flowers are pink when they first open but turn to white with age. When there is ample rainfall, the blooms appear again in the fall.

The bulb of the Wild Onion is much smaller than its dinnertable cousin, but it has a similar strong odor and is also kin to the garlic plant. Pretty Wild Onion flowers grow in bunches on short *stems* on the end of a larger stem. The plant usually grows to a height of ten inches. The flowers look like six pointed stars that have been shaped into small bells — they are about one-half inch across. The flower *stalks* grow taller than the slender, flat, blade-like leaves. After the flower is gone, small *bulblets* appear on the end of the stem. Although these little formations might not be considered beautiful, they sprout into interesting shapes as they develop.

A similar plant of the same family is the Crow Poison, but it does not have an "oniony" smell. The center of the Crow Poison is yellow.

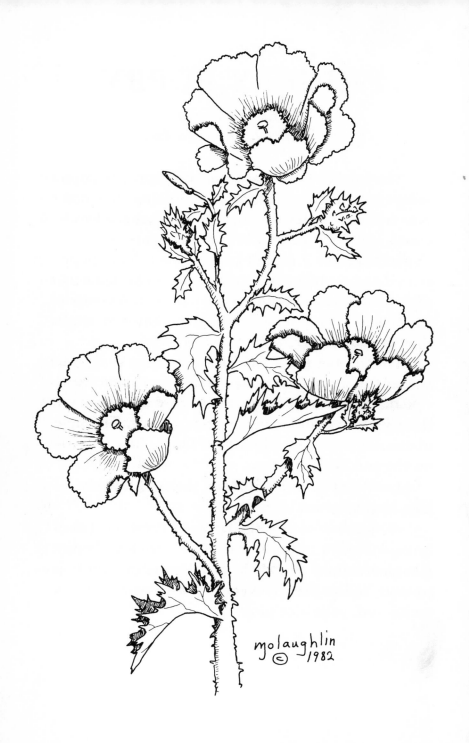

mclaughlin
© 1982

PRICKLY POPPY

Family: Poppy
Blooms: April into fall

The lovely white blossoms of the prickly poppy seem to be made of fragile tissue paper, but don't ever try to pick this wild beauty because the leaves, *stems* and buds are full of *spiny* stickers.

It would be a shame to pick the prickly poppy even if you could, because the *delicate* blossoms *wilt* almost as soon as they have been picked. As with all wildflowers, the blooms should be enjoyed where they grow.

The six petals of the blossom make a cup-like holder for the yellow *pollen* that is a favorite with visiting insects. The paper-thin flowers are about three inches across and the plant grows to a height of one and one-half to four feet. Single flowers grow on the end of the stems.

Leaves grow *alternately* on the stem and the foliage is gray-green in color.

A number of prickly poppies grow in Texas. Some of their names are Rose Prickly Poppy, Rough-stemmed Prickly Poppy, Texas Prickly Poppy and Yellow Prickly Poppy. The flowers may be white, red, yellow or pink.

QUEEN ANNE'S LACE

Family: Carrot
Blooms: June - July

It may seem surprising that *delicate* Queen Anne's Lace belongs to the same family as the rough-textured Eryngo, but it's true.

Queen Anne's Lace is well named because it does resemble fine, white lace. The flowers are only about one-eighth inch across and are *clustered* on short stems at the end of a sturdier stem. This type of growth is called an "umbel."

Although the individual flowers are tiny, the masses of white flowers in umbrella-like bunches can be quite showy. They grow along roadsides and in open fields — usually to heights of four feet. After the flowers are gone, fruit-bearing growth turns upward into a formation which looks like an umbrella that has been caught in the wind and turned inside out — ribs pointing upward.

It's easy to confuse Queen Anne's Lace with its look-alike cousin, wild carrot, but Queen Anne's Lace is a larger, taller, less common plant.

mplaughlin
©1982

RUELLIA

Family: Acanthus
Blooms: April - September

Although this flower is often called "wild petunia," it isn't a petunia at all but a member of the Acanthus Family. Perhaps it's called a "wild petunia," because it is *funnel* shaped and resembles the *cultivated* petunia, which is a member of the Potato Family.

Ruellias grow to a height of eight to twenty-four inches and are common in many parts of Texas. The flowers open in the morning and usually drop off the *stem* by afternoon. The funnel-shaped blooms have five deep *lobes* and are about two inches long and one and one-fourth inches across. The leaves grow opposite each other on the stem and are *lance* or *oval* shaped.

There are thirty-five kinds of ruellias in Texas and it is often difficult to tell them apart.

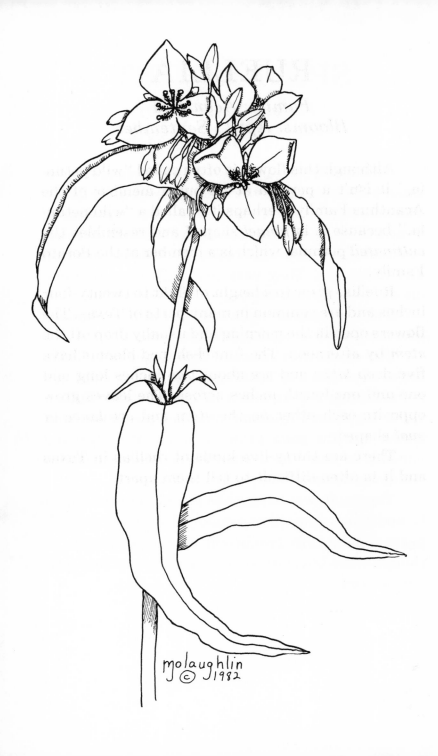

mclaughlin © 1982

SPIDERWORT

Family: Spiderwort
Blooms: April - May

This lovely three-petaled flower is easily recognized because no other flower is shaped quite like it. The soft blue or purple blossoms grow in groups of two or three on *stout stems*. Beneath the flowers are two leaf-like *bracts* which, like the leaves, are thin and blade like. They vary in length from five and one-half to thirteen inches.

The six stamens with their yellow tips of *pollen* give the flower a "spidery" appearance.

The spiderwort blossom lasts but a day. There are several kinds in Texas and identifying them can be confusing. One common variety is Prairie Spiderwort. Its flower is about one and one-half inches across and the plant grows to a height of two and one-half to three feet. Another common variety is Giant Spiderwort.

The dayflower belongs to the Spiderwort Family and looks somewhat similar. The dayflower appears to have only two bright blue upper petals, although there is a third smaller, lower petal that may not be seen.

mclaughlin
© 1982

THISTLE

Family: Composite
Blooms: March - May

There are many kinds of thistles and they have a special kind of rough-textured beauty although they are often called *"obnoxious weeds."* Thistles belong to the same family as the little fleabanes and asters. This is an example of how flower family members can be very different in appearance even though they are related.

Some common thistles *native* to Texas include Pasture Thistle, Texas Thistle, and Bull Thistle. All are full of *spiny* stickers, and their flowers look like small, bristly brushes turned up to the sky.

The flower pictured is a Bull Thistle which grows to a height of one to five feet. The bristly *disk flowers* are surrounded by *rosettes* of *spiny* leaf-like bracts. There are no petals or *ray flowers,* and several blossoms may grow on one *stem.*

The leaves of the Bull Thistle grow *alternately* on *stout* stems. The flowers may be pink, rose, purple, white or yellow. It grows in damp, open woods and on roadsides.

The blooming time given is for Bull Thistle. Other thistles bloom at different times.

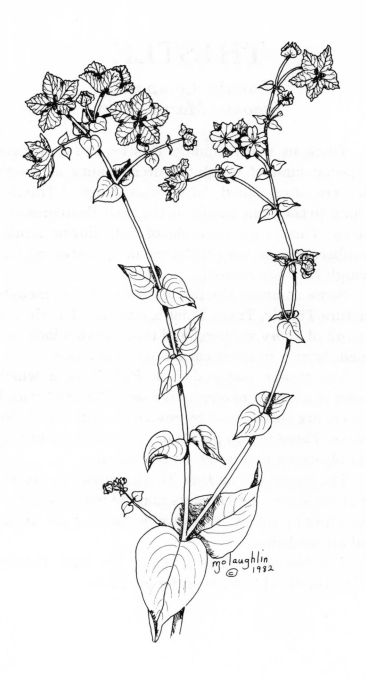

mc laughlin
© 1982

UMBRELLAWORT

Family: Four-o'clock
Blooms: April - May

The delicate bell-shaped pink flowers of the umbrellawort have no true petals but are formed of *sepals*. The flowers, as do other members of the Four-o'clock Family, open in the afternoon, blooming for only a short time. Soon after blooming, the flowers fall away leaving greenish umbrella-like *involucres* that are often mistaken for the flowers.

The umbrellawort grows to a height of one to three feet and the flowers are about one and one-half inches long. There are several *species* of umbrellawort and it is often difficult to tell them apart.

The leaves of the umbrellawort grow opposite each other and may be one to three inches long with uneven edges.

This flower resembles its *cultivated* cousin, the Garden Four-o'clock, although the umbrellawort is not as showy and colorful as the garden flower.

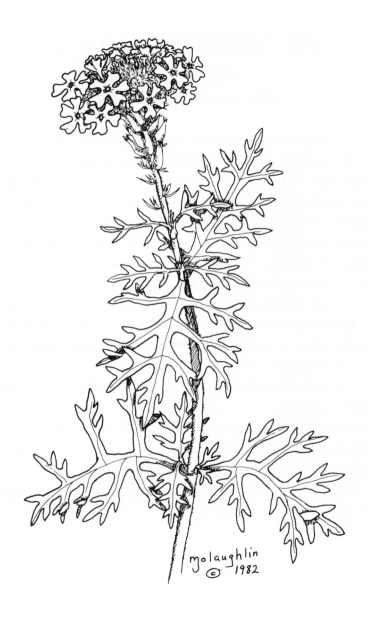

molaughlin © 1982

VERBENA

Family: Vervain
Blooms: Spring - Fall

There are thirty-four different kinds of verbena in Texas, but the Prairie Verbena (pictured) is perhaps the most common of all. It brightens roadsides and prairies throughout the state with varying shades of purple depending on soil conditions.

The blossom of the Prairie Verbena is a *cluster* of small flowers. They begin to bloom in early spring and continue until cold weather.

Each *floweret* in the cluster has four petals and is about one-half inch across. The flowerets are joined to the base by small tubes giving the appearance of a single blossom.

Prairie Verbena is a low-growing plant and is usually no taller than ten to twelve inches. The leaves grow opposite each other on the *stem* and are divided into thin *segments* which gives them a lacelike appearance.

Verbenas are easily grown and there are domestic varieties for home gardens.

mclaughlin
© 1982

WINE-CUP

Family: Mallow
Blooms: March - May

This flower looks exactly like it's name—a wine-red cup. The upright centers freely give their dusty *pollen* to every insect and breeze that ventures by, leaving a delicate frost on the dark petals. Another common name for this flower is poppy-mallow.

The leaves of the wine-cup grow alternately on the stem and are thin and on some *species* divided into three to five *segments*.

The flower of the wine-cup is about one and one-half to two and one-half inches across and the five petals are broad with toothed or *fringed* edges. The plant grows to a height of eight to twenty inches.

As with many plants, there are several kinds, or *species,* of wine-cups. The flowers look very much alike—the difference is often in the size of the plant and the *foliage.*

The wine-cup that grows most readily in the Blackland area of Texas has slender leaves and is a taller plant than the low-growing, fuzzy, broader-leaved species common in sandy land.

mclaughlin
© 1982

XANTHIUM SPECIOSUM

Family: Composite
Blooms: Fall

I could find no wildflower whose common name begins with "X" so in order to complete my *ABC's of Texas Wildflowers,* I looked for a *scientific name* beginning with that letter. All flowers and plants have scientific as well as common names.

Xanthium speciosum is the scientific name for "Cocklebur," and I decided this would be my "X" flower. This plant with funny looking spiny *burs,* belongs to the Composite Family, although it is difficult to imagine that Cockleburs are kin to daisies and asters. Hated by farmers and ranchers, Cockleburs are harmful to animals. The plant, leaves and all, is considered *poisonous,* but then it certainly doesn't look like anything that would be good to eat.

Cockleburs will stick to your clothes if you walk through the fields where they grow. They are also difficult to pull off of a pet's fur if the animal wanders too close when the burs are on the plant.

The plant grows to a height of three to five feet.

mclaughlin
© 1982

YAUPON

Family: Holly
Blooms: Spring

Yaupon Holly is a small *evergreen* tree or *shrub* that is better known for its bright red berries than for its small white flowers. Yaupon blooms in the spring; the berries appear in the fall. If not eaten by birds, the berries remain on the branches until the next flowering season. This is an excellent shrub for home gardens. Not all plants will have the beautiful berries, however, and it is well to make certain you are getting a berry-bearing yaupon if buying one from a nursery.

The woods of Central and East Texas wear Christmas colors with dark green leaves and scarlet berries if Yaupon Holly grows there. It's a holiday feast for birds because they prefer the berries of the yaupon to many other foods. As a tree, the yaupon may grow to a height of twenty-five feet.

The *native* holly of North Central Texas is the Deciduous or Possomhaw Holly which looks much like East Texas Yaupon with somewhat larger leaves and more orange color in the berries. The Deciduous Holly loses its leaves in winter which is the meaning of the word *"deciduous."*

mclaughlin
© 1982

ZEPHYRANTHES

Family: Amaryllis
Blooms: Late summer - Fall

Zephyranthes is a *scientific* name for "rain lily." I could find no common wildflower name beginning with "Z" so I looked through my books until I found *Zephyranthes.* Although this scientific name is less frequently used today, it was once fairly common. There are several kinds of *Zephyranthes* and the one pictured is the common, small rain lily or Drummond's Rain Lily.

This little creamy white, six-petaled flower seems to pop up out of nowhere a few days after a rain. There are no leaves or plant to tell that a flower *bulb* is underground until the rain awakens the plant, and a single flower appears on a long, thin stem.

After the rain, if the weather is sunny, the flower usually lasts but a day; but if the weather is cloudy, the blossom may last a few days longer.

The pretty white blossom is about two inches long and one and one-fourth inches across.

GLOSSARY

Although these words may have several other meanings, we have given only those that apply to wildflowers.

Abundance: A great number; growing in profusion.

Alternately: Arranged at different levels on a stem. Not across from each other.

Blade: The broad, flat part of a leaf or petal.

Bract: A *modified* leaf growing around or under a flower.

Bulb: A large underground bud covered with layers of thick, fleshy, scale-like leaves. Example: onion.

Bulblet: Small bulb.

Bur: A rough or prickly flower head or seed-case.

Characteristic: Special quality or appearance of flower that makes it different from others.

Chaff: External covering of seed.

Cluster: A group of flowers, leaves or other plant parts.

Composite: Of several parts. Also the name of a flower family.

Compound leaf: One that has several leaflets growing from a single stem.

Coarse: Made up of large parts; not fine.

Cultivate: To produce or improve plants; to care for in order to grow stronger, healthier plants.

Deciduous: Having leaves that fall off at the end of the growing season.

Devour: To consume or eat greedily.

Disk flowers: Small flowers in the center of the flowerhead of members of the Composite Family.

Delicate: Fragile, easily bruised or broken.

Domestic plant: One that has been cultivated from a wild plant into a more easily grown, useful or beautiful plant.

Escape: For a garden-type plant or flower to come up somewhere else as a wild plant without cultivation.

Evergreen plant: One that does not lose its leaves at the end of the growing season. The opposite of deciduous.

Floral: Flower like.

Flower: Blossom, bloom. Part of a plant that contains stamen and pistil — reproductive organs of a plant. Both are usually present in a flower but not always.

Floweret: Small flower.

Flowerhead: A dense cluster of tiny flowers growing from a single stem of the Composite Family.

Foliage: The leaves of a plant or tree.

Forage: Food suitable for horses, cattle or other domestic or wild animals.

Fork: To divide into two or more parts.

Fragile: Delicate. Easily broken or bruised.

Fringed: Having an ornamental border or edge.

Funnel: A utensil with a wide mouth tapering to a narrow tube or opening.

Hue: The color or shade of a color.

Identify: To recognize; to be able to name a flower correctly.

Involucre: A whorl of bracts underneath a flower as in the umbrellawort.

Lance shaped: Shaped like a lance or spear; longer than it is wide with tapering pointed ends.

Leaflet: Small leaf usually growing in a cluster. A part of a compound leaf.

Lobe: Rounded projection or division as "the lobe of a leaf."

Modify: To change or alter in some way.

Native plant: A species of plant which occurs naturally in a certain area without having been brought in by people.

Naturalize: To escape cultivation; to grow wild in an area in which the plant is not native.

Nodule: A small knot or node.

Notched: Having a "v" shape.

Nutrient: Something that nourishes; food.

Oblong: Longer than wide.

Obnoxious: Anything that is objectionable, disagreeable or unpleasant.

Oval: Egg shaped.

Ovule: The part of the plant contained in the ovary that, when fertilized, becomes a seed.

Opposite: Across from each other.

Pistil: The female reproductive organ of a flower that consists of stigma, style, and ovary. The ovary contains ovules which, when fertilized by pollen grains, become seeds.

Poisonous: A poisonous plant or substance is one that, if eaten, can injure or kill a living thing.

Pollen: Grains born by the anther (see stamen) which fertilize the ovule beginning reproduction.

Pungent: Having a strong odor.

Quinine: A bitter drug used to treat malaria and other diseases.

Raceme: An elongated stem with many flowers growing on short stems from it. Those at the bottom usually open first. Example: bluebonnet.

Ray flower: Outer petal-like flower in the flowerhead of the Composite Family.

Rosette: Something resembling the petals of a rose. A cluster of leaves or flowers growing in this way.

Saw-toothed: With points like a saw edge.

Scale: Anything layered resembling the scale of a fish, as one of the tiny leaves that protect a bud.

Sepal: One segment of a *calyx* which is the outer whorl of a flower.

Species: A group of plants resembling each other in most ways. The plants in the species will have more differences with other plants in the larger family group.

Spine: A sharp outgrowth of the stem or of a leaf or fruit.

Sprout: To begin to grow.

Stamen: The part of a flower that bears the pollen. It has two parts: filament and anther.

Stem: Main part of a plant that supports the flower, leaves or fruit: a stalk.

Stigma: The part of the pistil that receives pollen causing seeds to develop into flowers.

Stout: Strong, sturdy.

Style: That part of the pistil between the ovary and stigma; it sometimes looks like a stalk. All flowers do not have a style. (See pistil)

Tinged: Having a faint trace of color. Not brightly colored.

Umbel: A flowering stalk with shorter stems growing from a larger stem giving an umbrella-like appearance.

Weed: Any unsightly, common or troublesome plant that grows in abundance.

Whorl: A row of leaves or flowers surrounding a stem.

Wildflower: The flower of an uncultivated plant; one that grows from seeds that occur in nature and are not planted by a person.

Wilt: To droop or become limp; to lose freshness.

FLOWER FAMILIES

These are listed in the order in which they first appear in the book. Although there are twenty-six flowers, there are only sixteen families because some of the flowers belong to the same family. The flowers listed after the family name are those that are in the book.

COMPOSITE FAMILY (aster, cone-flower, fleabane, goldenrod, Indian Blanket, Mexican Hat, thistle, *Xanthium*)

This is the largest flower family in Texas — in fact in the United States. It includes plants such as daisies, sunflowers, dandelions, ragweeds and Cockleburs. Many of our garden flowers belong to this family, such as, chrysanthemums, dahlias, and zinnias. Some members find their way to the dinner table because lettuce, endive and artichokes are Composites.

Composites usually have many flowers within one *flower-head*. The center of the flower is made up of small flowers called *disk flowers*. The outer *ray flowers* are also called petals.

LEGUME FAMILY (bluebonnet)

Members of this family have beans or *legumes* as their fruit. The bean is usually divided into two equal parts with a coat or pod that splits down the middle when it is ripe. There may be many or only a few seeds within the pod. Examine a bean served for dinner and you will discover that it too belongs to this family — there are wild and *domestic* members.

Most members of this family have *compound* leaves. Look at the leaf of a bluebonnet and you will understand this type of leaf arrangement. There are varying numbers of *leaflets* — the bluebonnet has five.

Many members of the Legume Family have flowers that grow on a *raceme*. The flowerets often have five petals, the largest three arranged so that they look like a small face. Most flowers in this family seem to have "flower faces."

DOGWOOD FAMILY (dogwood)

There are several kinds of dogwood — most are small trees or shrubs — a few grow as small herbs. The one described in the book is Flowering, or Eastern, Dogwood. Among other members of the family are Japanese Dogwood and Pacific Dogwood. These members also have white or yellowish *bracts* that surround small flowers.

Another member of the family, however — Rough-leaf Dogwood — has four true petals. It grows to a height of fifteen feet and looks very much like Flowering Dogwood and is *native* to some areas of Texas.

CARROT FAMILY (eryngo, Queen Anne's Lace)

There are about forty-two members of the Carrot Family, also called the Parsley Family, that grow in Texas. Most of the flowers of this family are arranged in *umbels* — small flowers growing on short stems attached to a larger *stalk*. They look like umbrellas. The flowers are small and inconspicious but can be quite showy as a group. The leaves of plants in this family are much divided and some like those of the eryngo have sharp-pointed tips.

As with all plant families, there are small groups within the family that are more closely related to each other. These smaller groups are called *species*. There are at least two species of eryngo and several species of wild carrot, one of which is Queen Anne's Lace.

Although some members of this family are eaten as vegetables, other members are very *poisonous*.

MINT FAMILY (horsemint)

If you are familiar with such flavors as "peppermint" and "spearmint" then you know something about this family — that many of its members have strong, pungent odors. Not all are as sweet as peppermint, however. Mints are often cultivated for their oil and used in flavorings and medicine (menthol).

Members of the Mint Family have interesting common names such as Skull Cap, Rattlesnake Flower, Lionheart, Heal-all, Henbit, and Scarlet Sage. Horsemints are a coarser, less delicate, flower than many of the other Mints. Almost all Mints have a square (four-sided) stem.

LOGANIA FAMILY (jasmine)

Members of this family often have five joined petals on each flower as does the Jasmine described in the book. Many members are tropical plants but several kinds are found in Texas. The leaves usually grow from the stem as pairs. Names of Logania Family members are Indian Pink, Hornpod, Wand Hornpod and Juniper Leaf.

EVENING PRIMROSE FAMILY (kisses)

Most flowers in this family have four broad petals, one on each side of the flower. They may be white, pink or yellow. Some of their names are Pink Evening Primrose, Day Primrose and Fluttermill. It is sometimes difficult to tell one kind from the other in this group of Evening Primroses.

Other members of this family look quite different from the others. One such member is kisses described in the book. Small flowers bloom along a *spike* with two or three of the *flowerets* blooming at one time. The four petals are grouped toward one side of the flower, while the pistil and stamens are on the other side.

VERVAIN FAMILY (verbena, lantana)

This is a large family with some of the members, like Prairie Verbena, growing throughout Texas. Most of the Vervains have small flowers with *lobed* petals (usually five) growing in flat clusters at the top of the stem. Other members have flowers which grow on spikes. Slender Vervain, a common roadside flower, is such a member.

POTATO FAMILY (nightshade)

Some members of this family are good to eat. These include potatoes, tomatoes, green peppers, and egg plants. Almost all of the wildflowers belonging to the Potato Family are very poisonous, however.

Many of the plants of the Potato Family are unpleasant to

touch having rough, hairy leaves and spiny branches. Some, like the Buffalo Bur, have berries covered with sharp-pointed spines. The Ground Cherry is an interesting member of this family. The seeds of this plant are carried in small balloon or lantern-like containers.

LILY FAMILY (Wild Onion)

This large family has many beautiful members. Most of the flowers have six petals and blade-like leaves. Some of the plants have no leaves at all during their blooming season.

The lovely little Dogtooth Violet is quite different from the tall, creamy blossom of the yucca. Both belong to the Lily Family. Wild Onion, Wild Garlic and Crow Poison are three of the most common members of the family.

POPPY FAMILY (prickly poppy)

Most members of this family have lovely, *delicate,* wide-open blossoms that invite passing insects to visit the store of *pollen.* But many of the poppies have sharp-pointed leaves that discourage anyone who might want to pick the *fragile* flowers.

SPIDERWORT FAMILY (spiderwort)

Members of this family are easy to *identify.* There are two groups within the family: dayflowers and spiderworts. Dayflowers have three petals but the upper petals are so much larger than the bottom one, that it is often considered a two-petaled flower. There are several kinds of dayflowers, all have bright blue petals.

Other members of the family are called "spiderworts." The three petals of this flower are the same size. The flowers may be shades of purple or blue.

Leaves of all members of the Spiderwort Family are long and blade like.

FOUR-O'CLOCK FAMILY (umbrellawort)

This family was given its name because the flowers of most of its members open at about four o'clock in the afternoon. The flowers have no petals but grow as small *funnels.* The most common member is the Four o'Clock. The bright red flowers are open for only a short time.

The Umbrellawort, described in the book, is also called

Pink Four o'Clock. Its flowers are also short lived. When they fall off, they leave a pale green *involucre* surrounding the stem that is often mistaken for the flower.

MALLOW FAMILY (wine cup)

This is a large family with thousands of members. They grow as low plants, shrubs or trees. Cotton and okra are members of this family.

Most mallows have five petals on each blossom and the *stamens* hold the *pollen* above the center so that it is available to passing insects. Some other members of the Mallow Family are Poppy Mallow, Rose Mallow, Turk's Cap and Velvet Leaf.

HOLLY FAMILY (Yaupon)

Members of the Holly Family grow as small trees or shrubs. All have red, yellow or orange berries and small inconspicuous flowers. Some Holly names are Inkberry, American, Carolina and Winterberry.

AMARYLLIS FAMILY (*Zephyranthes*)

It's hard to believe that the tall century plant belongs to the same family as the little *Zephyranthes* or rain lily described in the book. Other members in the family are Copper Lily, Yellow Star Grass and Spider Lily. Daffodils also belong to the Amaryllis Family, but there are few if any wild daffodils in Texas.

Members of this family have six-petaled flowers.

BIBLIOGRAPHY

Ajilvsgi, Geyata. 1979. *Wild Flowers of the Big Thicket, East Texas and Western Louisiana.* College Station: Texas A & M University Press.

Rickett, H. W. 1969. *Wildflowers of the United States. Texas.* New York: McGraw-Hill. (out of print)

Whitehouse, Eula. 1967. *Texas Flowers in Natural Color.* 3rd edition. Dallas: Dallas County Audubon Society.

Wills, M. M. and H. S. Irwin. 1961. *Roadside Flowers of Texas.* Austin. University of Texas Press.

THE AUTHOR

Glenna Grimmer has been known for fifteen years as "The Bird Lady" because of her beautiful bird carvings. Now she has extended her interest to include all of nature, and she wants to help others, particularly children, find the joy that she has discovered through her study of wildflowers. Well-known as an artist, writer, photographer, and platform speaker, her works have been purchased by banks, libraries, and museums and are in private collections throughout the United States. Glenna and her husband live in Farmers Branch and her studio-gallery, The Bird Nest, is in Carrollton.

THE ARTIST

Mary Jo Laughlin has received high acclaim as a wildflower artist. Her paintings have a detailed clarity that makes them both horticulturally accurate and artistically beautiful. She works primarily in watercolor, sketching her subjects in the fields where they grow then adding true-to-life color later in her studio. She has been painting wildflowers for twelve years, and her paintings are in collections throughout the nation. Mary Jo lives in McKinney where her husband is Administrative Director of Heard Natural Science Museum.

08430079